SHARK!

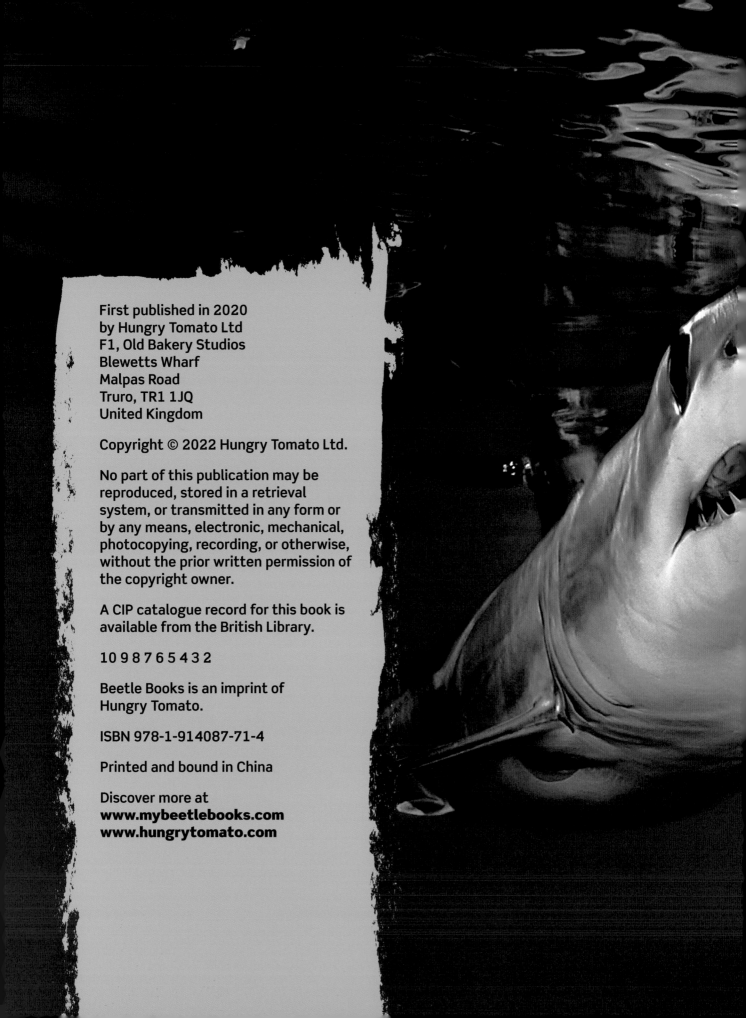

First published in 2020
by Hungry Tomato Ltd
F1, Old Bakery Studios
Blewetts Wharf
Malpas Road
Truro, TR1 1JQ
United Kingdom

A CIP catalogue record for this book is
available from the British Library.

10 9 8 7 6 5 4 3 2

Beetle Books is an imprint of
Hungry Tomato.

ISBN 978-1-914087-71-4

Printed and bound in China

Discover more at
www.mybeetlebooks.com
www.hungrytomato.com

SHARK!

by Paul Mason

CONTENTS

1. HOW SHARKS HUNT

SHARKS: APEX PREDATORS

Most big sharks are apex predators, scared of nothing. They are eating machines. Almost everything about sharks is designed for catching and consuming food.

The bull shark will eat just about anything that comes its way—including humans, but very rarely. Fortunately, it *usually* eats fish.

BULL SHARK

Unlike most sharks, bull sharks can survive in **fresh water**. Some live full-time in a lake in Australia, having swum there during a flood!

Bull sharks are common in shallow water near the coast. They sometimes gather in packs.

The goblin shark is sometimes called a "living fossil." It is the last survivor of a family of sharks that first appeared roughly 100 million years ago.

SHARKS EVERYWHERE

Our oceans are full of sharks. Wherever there is prey to eat, you find sharks hunting. Down in the gloom of the deep oceans, for instance, lurks the goblin shark. Below the Arctic ice you might spot a Greenland shark. And lying camouflaged on the seabed off shores around the world are various species of angel shark.

WOLVES OF THE SEA

Sharks are sometimes called "wolves of the sea." This name started with blue sharks. It came from their habit of gathering in packs, then attacking when they found something that could be a meal. Blue sharks are not that fussy about what they eat—in 1942, one was even caught with a bottle of wine in its stomach!

SHARK SCIENCE: SHARK-AEOLOGY

Fossil discoveries show that sharks have been around for a long time. Shark ancestors first appeared over 400 million years ago. Modern humans, *Homo sapiens*, only appeared less than 200,000 years ago!

WHAT SHARKS EAT

There are about 450 shark species. Some will eat whatever they find, others hunt one specific kind of prey. Most sharks prefer to eat other fish.

SHARKS THAT EAT JUST ABOUT ANYTHING

Many big species, such as tiger sharks, bull sharks, blue sharks, and great white sharks, eat all kinds of things. They have all been found with strange items in their stomachs—including a suit of armor. (Experts are not 100% certain this story is true. It was recorded in the 1500s by a **naturalist** called Guillaume Rondelet.)

TIGER SHARK

CRAZY CONTENTS OF TIGER SHARK TUMMIES

Tiger sharks are nicknamed the "garbage cans of the sea." These are just a few of the crazy things that have been found in their stomachs:

- An echidna (an Australian animal similar to a porcupine)
- A bag of money
- A chicken coop—with chickens inside
- Tom-tom drums
- A car license plate

NOT ON THE MENU: HUMAN

One thing sharks DON'T eat is humans—or not very often. Only a few shark species have ever attacked people. For us, the most dangerous are the great white, bull shark, and tiger shark. A few others have bitten people, but attacks on humans are almost always a case of mistaken identity.

Tiger sharks are not fussy eaters. This one is nibbling on some tasty camera equipment.

PICKY EATERS

Some sharks are adapted to eat special types of food. Basking sharks, whale sharks, and a species called the megamouth hoover up tiny plankton and krill with their giant mouths. Mako and blue sharks use their great speed to catch fast-moving fish. Angel and zebra horn sharks even eat shellfish!

SHARK SCIENCE:
WHAT IS A SHARK?

Things that make sharks different from other fish:

- Their skeleton is made of tough **cartilage**, not bone.
- They can only swim forward, and many have to keep swimming all the time to keep breathing.
- Their teeth are in rows, which are always pushing forward to replace teeth that have been lost.

This angel shark is settling back on the seabed with a small fish in its mouth.

FINDING PREY

A fish or sea mammal that is bleeding is almost certain to attract sharks. Many sharks follow the smell of blood to find possible prey.

The part of a shark's brain used for smell is large. Sharks can follow a smell for hundreds of yards.

Sharks use special sensors on the underside of their snout to pick up smells. The sensors are called nares, and there is one on each side of the shark's snout.

Water flows into the hole at the top, and out of the bottom.

LEMON SHARK

A shark can tell where a smell comes from. If the smell reaches its right nare before the left one, the shark knows the smell is coming from the right.

Sniffing out prey

It is not only the blood of wounded animals that sharks can smell. They can also sniff out healthy prey. According to the American Museum of Natural History, lemon sharks can detect just a teaspoon of fish oil in a swimming pool of water.

Some sharks, such as this blind shark, have barbels hanging down from their snouts. These are used to locate prey.

Vibrations in the water

Sharks also detect prey from the sounds and vibrations made by struggling or injured fish. Sharks have ears at the sides of their head, though there is only a tiny hole on the outside. But they also have a much bigger system for sensing vibrations in the water. This is called the "lateral line."

Shark science: *The Lateral Line*

The lateral line is a line of sensors under a shark's skin, running down the side of its body.

Along the line, a gel-like substance wobbles whenever the water is disturbed. The wobbles trigger a message to the shark's brain. It says: *Something worth investigating is happening!*

HUNTING BY SIGHT

Sight is an important hunting tool for many sharks. Once they are close enough to see their prey, they use vision to close in for the kill.

This great white was moving so fast it left the water completely—and did a front flip!

ATTACKING FROM BELOW

Great white sharks rely on vision when attacking from below. When it is ready, the great white races straight up to the surface and hits the prey at full speed.

The shark swims underneath its prey, which is usually a seal.

The seal is outlined against the light above, and easy to see.

The seal is unlikely to spot the shark in the gloom below.

Seals are often stunned by the force of a great white's attack.

GREAT WHITE SHARK

Down here on the seabed, this seal is safe from attack. Unfortunately, though, she has to go up to the surface to breathe.

Great whites are thought to be able to swim at up to 25 mph (40 km/h).

HUNTING AT NIGHT

Sharks have good vision in darkness. They can make the most of any available light. Hunting at night, dusk, or dawn is no problem. For the great white, this is a big advantage. Seals—which are its main prey—travel to their feeding grounds at night and return at dawn. Most other sharks also hunt at night.

SLEEPING SHARKS

Most sharks have to keep moving to breathe. They need a constant stream of water through their gills. Some sharks, though, are able to pump water while lying on the sea bottom. One of these is the sand tiger or gray nurse shark. After a tough night's hunting, sand tigers lie on the bottom and rest for the day!

SHARK SCIENCE:
THE TAPETUM LUCIDUM

The reason sharks see well without much light is the *tapetum lucidum*. This is a special layer in their eyes, behind the **retina**.

The *tapetum lucidum* works by reflecting light back to the retina. This means the retina gets extra light signals, so the shark can see better in the gloom.

The photographer's light has lit up the *tapetum lucidum* of this bigeye houndshark.

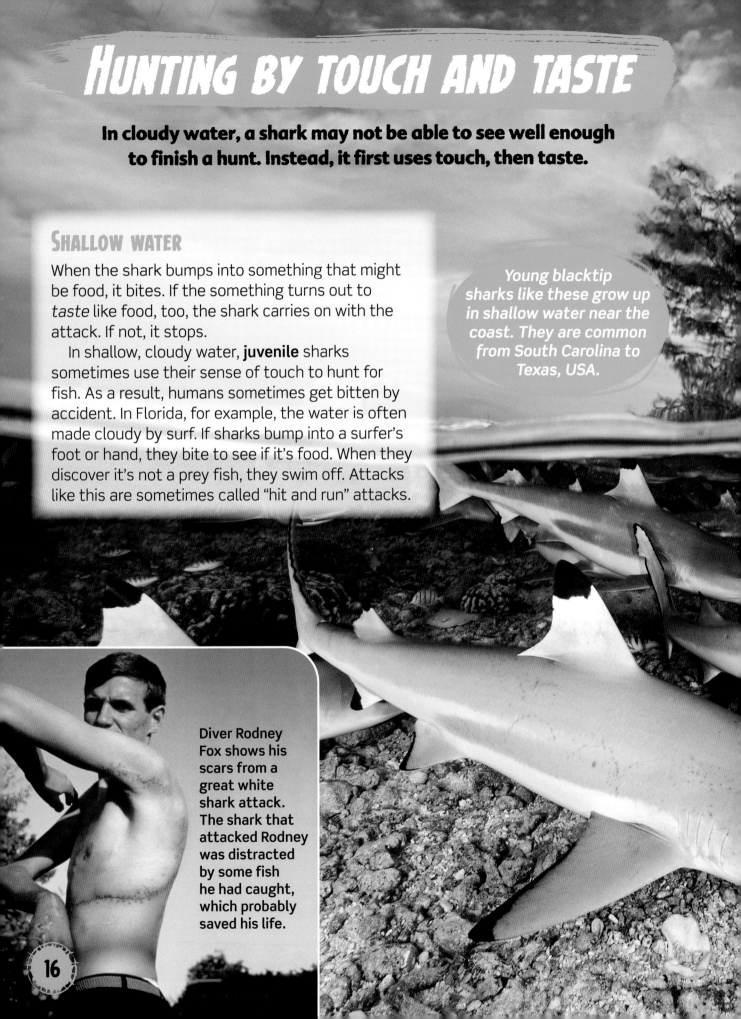

HUNTING BY TOUCH AND TASTE

In cloudy water, a shark may not be able to see well enough to finish a hunt. Instead, it first uses touch, then taste.

SHALLOW WATER

When the shark bumps into something that might be food, it bites. If the something turns out to *taste* like food, too, the shark carries on with the attack. If not, it stops.

In shallow, cloudy water, **juvenile** sharks sometimes use their sense of touch to hunt for fish. As a result, humans sometimes get bitten by accident. In Florida, for example, the water is often made cloudy by surf. If sharks bump into a surfer's foot or hand, they bite to see if it's food. When they discover it's not a prey fish, they swim off. Attacks like this are sometimes called "hit and run" attacks.

Young blacktip sharks like these grow up in shallow water near the coast. They are common from South Carolina to Texas, USA.

Diver Rodney Fox shows his scars from a great white shark attack. The shark that attacked Rodney was distracted by some fish he had caught, which probably saved his life.

16

BUMP AND BITE

Large sharks also use touch and taste to see if something is food. These sharks, though, bump into things with their snouts on purpose.

First the shark circles an interesting object. Then it swims up from behind and either bumps it or takes a test bite. If the object is edible—even if it is a human—a large shark may continue the attack. This style of hunting is called "bump and bite." Great whites and bull sharks are known to hunt in this way.

SHARK SCIENCE: TOUCH-SENSITIVE TEETH

Sharks have lots of nerves in their skin that can sense touch. They also have touch-sensitive teeth.

Sharks obviously do not have hands to feel with. Instead, they use their teeth to investigate unknown objects. They sometimes start with what is a nibble to them (it would not feel like a nibble to you!). Then they may bite harder.

BLACKTIP SHARKS

ELECTRO-LOCATION

Electro-location is a shark's secret weapon in its hunt for prey. Even if it cannot smell, hear, see, or touch its prey, electro-location helps the shark find something to eat.

This great hammerhead is swimming along using its hammer like a metal detector. It is not looking for buried treasure—it's trying to sense stingrays buried in the sand.

FINDING PREY WITH ELECTRICITY

Electro-location uses tiny holes underneath a shark's snout, called the ampullae of Lorenzini. These let the shark sense anything nearby that is producing electricity. Even the tiny electrical force of a fish's heartbeat shows up.

In many sharks, the ampullae are most tightly packed near their mouth. This helps the shark sense its prey's final attempts to escape. Hammerhead sharks have the ultimate electro-location tools. Their wide snouts have space for thousands of ampullae.

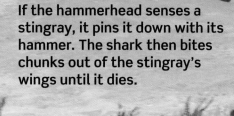

A buried stingray's body will give off tiny electrical pulses.

If the hammerhead senses a stingray, it pins it down with its hammer. The shark then bites chunks out of the stingray's wings until it dies.

This stingray is trying to hide in the sand—but he'd better hope a hammerhead doesn't come along.

SHARK DETERRENT!

For years people have wondered how to stop shark attacks. One way to do this is said to be by carrying a special device that gives off an electric field. Nine times out of 10, when the shark gets close, it senses the field and turns away.

For goblin sharks, as for other deepwater sharks, electro-location is one of the most important hunting tools.

HAMMERHEAD SHARK

Some hammerheads have been found with almost 100 stingray **barbs** in their hammers. It seems the stingray's sting does not bother the shark.

SHARK SCIENCE: AMPULLAE OF LORENZINI

The ampullae of Lorenzini are gel-filled **pores** in a shark's snout. The pores are lined with tiny, sensitive cells.

The electric field from other animals in the water is transmitted to the gel, and the cells detect it. They send a message that there is something alive right under the shark's nose.

HIGH-SPEED ATTACKERS

Some sharks target fast-swimming prey, such as tuna. Bluefin tuna can swim at over 35 mph (60 km/h)! To catch them, sharks have to be speedy, too.

THE SPEEDIEST SHARK

The fastest shark of all is the shortfin mako, which hunts bluefish, tuna, and mackerel. It is difficult to measure a shark's speed, but it's claimed that makos can swim at over 43 mph (70 km/h). They sometimes travel so fast that they leap clear of the water. Makos have been reported jumping 30 ft (9 m)—almost as high as the highest diving platform at the Olympic Games.

Compared to other sharks, the mako has a much larger tail relative to its body. This allows it to generate lots of speed.

SWIFT ATTACKS

Although the shortfin mako is the fastest shark, many others use speed in the final phase of an attack. After the mako, the next fastest sharks are the great white and the blue shark. Each of these is thought to be able to reach 25 mph (40 km/h) in short bursts of speed.

Like the mako, the blue shark has a long, slim shape designed for speed.

The jaw is longer than it is wide, which is good for grabbing fish at high speed.

SHORTFIN MAKO SHARK

The **dorsal fin** stops the shark rolling as it swims and helps it change direction.

Compare the mako with the tiger shark on page 10. The mako's body is long and pointed, enabling it to shoot through the water like an arrow.

The dorsal fin and swept-back **pectoral fins** are low-drag, so they do not slow the mako down.

SHARK SCIENCE: HYDRODYNAMICS

Hydrodynamics is the science of how water flows. It is similar to aerodynamics, the science of air flow.

Aerodynamics says that a sleek supercar will be faster than a flat-fronted van. In the same way, a sleek shark is faster than a big, wide one.

SHARK AMBUSHES

Few sharks hunt mainly by sight. The angel shark, though, lies in wait until it sees prey swimming past. Then, quick as a flash, it strikes!

A BIG FAMILY

There are about 20 members of the angel shark family, but they all hunt in a similar way. Their wide, flat bodies are perfect for lying camouflaged or hidden on the seabed. They wait in ambush until prey swims past. You can see how an angel shark lies in wait on the opposite page.

LIGHTNING-FAST STRIKE

Once its ambush is ready, the angel shark waits until a fish comes just close enough. Sometimes the wait can last days. When a fish does swim within range, though, the angel shark's strike is almost too fast to see. Less than a tenth of a second after the attack has been launched, the fish is in the shark's mouth.

When hunting, the angel shark lies on the sandy seabed.

An angel shark's skin is just the right shade to camouflage it in the sand.

The dorsal fins and tail lie flat, so that nothing sticks up to warn prey.

The shark wriggles down, hiding at least the edges of its body.

For a shark that relies on its vision to find prey, hunting at night seems an impossible challenge. But if no food comes along in daytime, the angel shark isn't defeated. It hunts at night using bioluminescence, the light trail created by fish as they swim.

Sometimes the shark covers itself almost completely, so that only its eyes and part of its head are exposed.

ANGEL SHARK

SHARK SCIENCE: *BIOLUMINESCENCE*

Bioluminescence is light given off by some living things. It is the result of a chemical reaction.

The bodies of some fish are bioluminescent. Others leave a bioluminescent trail. As they swim along, these fish disturb tiny organisms in the water. The organisms give off bioluminescent light.

JAWS OF DEATH

Sharks' jaws are not like those of other animals. Their jaws work in a way that lets them take a MUCH bigger bite than you would expect. In fact, some sharks' jaws open almost as high and wide as their own bodies.

A shark's upper jaw is not solidly attached to its skull, as it is in most other animals.

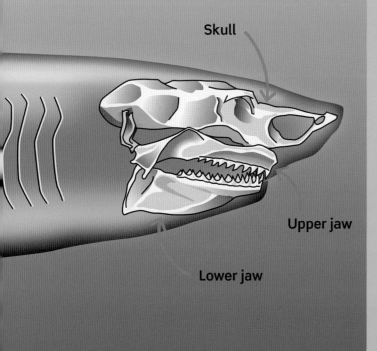

Skull

Upper jaw

Lower jaw

As it prepares to bite, the shark lifts its snout and opens its lower jaw, opening its mouth wide.

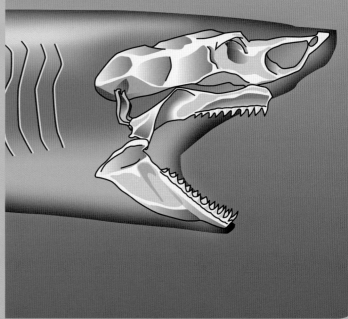

Instead of using its jaws, the sawshark slashes its saw from side to side in the sediment on the seabed to get prey.

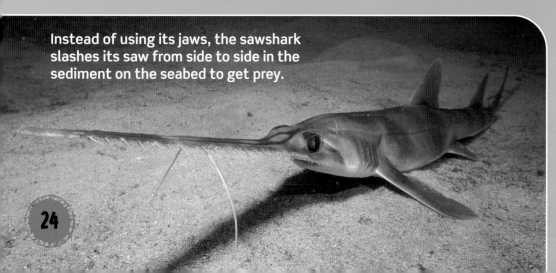

Big mouths with no bite

Not all sharks have a fearsome bite like a great white's. Two of the biggest—the whale shark and basking shark—have huge mouths that rarely bite anything. Along with the incredibly rare megamouth shark, they are the only planktivorous sharks. This means that they live mainly off tiny sea creatures called plankton, which they scoop up in their huge mouths.

A giant basking shark gulps down plankton while swimming lazily along.

The shark's upper jaw then moves away from its skull and pushes forward. This makes an even bigger bite. In some sharks, the opening movement sucks in water, dragging prey into their mouth.

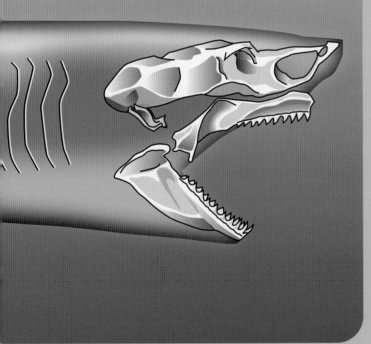

The upper and lower jaws snap together. A great white's bite is about as powerful as a lion's (and three times as strong as a human's), but its sharp teeth do massive damage.

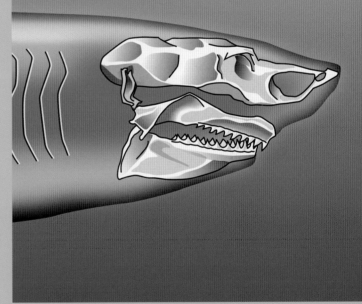

SHARK SCIENCE: BITE ID

When you bite into something, it leaves behind a pattern called a bite mark.

Every shark species has a different bite mark. The size and shape of their jaws and the position of their teeth are like a species fingerprint. A shark expert can often identify a shark just from its bite mark.

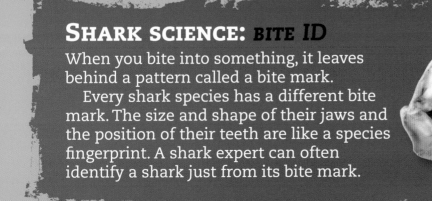

Shark migrations

A migration is a journey from one feeding place to another. For some sharks, their whole life is a migration in search of food.

One of the great shark migrations happens when sharks follow sardine **shoals** up the coast of south-east Africa.

Regular migrations

Some sharks return to the same places every year to hunt for food. Off the coast of southern Africa, for example, huge sardine shoals appear every June. The sharks know the sardines are coming, and make sure they are waiting. In fact sharks, dolphins, seabirds, and whales ALL come to feast on the sardines.

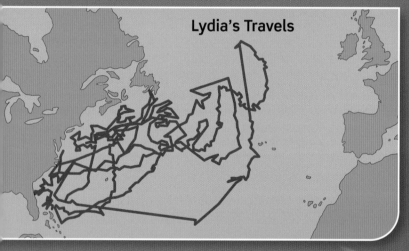
Lydia's Travels

Constant motion

Some sharks are always on the move in search of food. They cover huge distances. In 2014, for example, a female great white was tagged off the coast of Florida, USA. Lydia, as she was called, headed off along the east coast of North America. Then she set off across the Atlantic Ocean.

A year after being tagged, Lydia was in the eastern Atlantic, heading towards Cornwall in the UK. She had swum more than 18,500 miles (30,000 km).

Groups of sharks circle the ball of sardines. Bronze whalers, dusky sharks, silky sharks, and blacktip sharks are among the species that will attack the **bait ball**.

The sardines pack themselves together in a constantly moving ball. This makes it hard for predators to pick out a fish to attack.

SHARK SCIENCE: NAVIGATION

How do sharks find their way around? Scientists have several theories:

- Some, such as tiger sharks, seem to use the Earth's magnetic field as a kind of shark satnav.
- Other sharks may have a good memory of the area they inhabit.
- Sharks may also use ocean currents and water temperatures to tell them where they are.

SHARK IDENTIFICATION

Scientists classify sharks in different groups according to their physical characteristics. This flow chart will help you identify some of the most commonly seen types of shark:

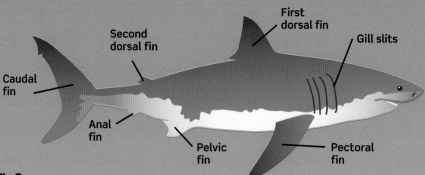

Does the shark have an anal fin?

Yes   No

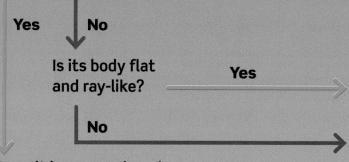

Is its body flat and ray-like?

Yes → It's one of 22 different species of **angel shark**.

No → It's a **dogfish shark**.

Does it have one dorsal fin and six or seven pairs of gill slits?

Yes → It's a **cow shark**, such as a bluntnose sixgill or sharpnose sevengill shark.

No

Does it have dorsal fins with spines on them?

Yes → It's a **bullhead shark**. There are only nine species, including the horn shark and the Port Jackson and zebra bullhead sharks.

No

Is its mouth in front of its eyes?

Yes → It's a **carpet shark**. Members of this group are quite different in size: it includes giant whale sharks and little bamboo sharks.

No

Does it have a nictitating eyelid (an extra eyelid that closes for protection)?

Yes → It's one of nearly 300 different species of **ground shark**. This group includes dangerous sharks such as tiger and bull sharks, as well as tiny, harmless catsharks.

No → It's a **mackerel shark**, a group that includes the great white and mako sharks.

2. THE WORLD'S WEIRDEST SHARKS

FRILLED SHARK

The frilled shark looks like something from a horror movie. With over 300 teeth, it's a good job it only grows about 6 ft 6 in (2 m) long and lives in the deep oceans.

DEEP-OCEAN HUNTER

The frilled shark has been recorded over 0.9 miles (1.5 km) below the ocean surface. Light does not reach this far down, so the shark hunts in darkness. It likes "upwellings": places where cold, deep water moves upwards. Here, plankton—and the fish that hunt the plankton—are common.

Old stories of sea serpents may have been based on frilled sharks. Sailors who caught one by accident would never have seen anything like it.

When it senses prey, the frilled shark strikes quickly.

AN ANCIENT SPECIES

The frilled shark rarely comes close to the surface, so few have ever been seen. In fact, this shark is so rare that it was only officially discovered in 2004. This is not a new shark species, though. Scientists know it has been hunting in the deep oceans for at least 95 million years. Based on **fossil** evidence, some experts think it may have been down there for three times that long.

The frilled shark's most horrifying feature is its mouthful of teeth.

As it strikes, the shark closes its gills, creating a suction effect that pulls prey on to its teeth.

Every row of teeth points back towards the shark's throat, making it almost impossible for prey to escape.

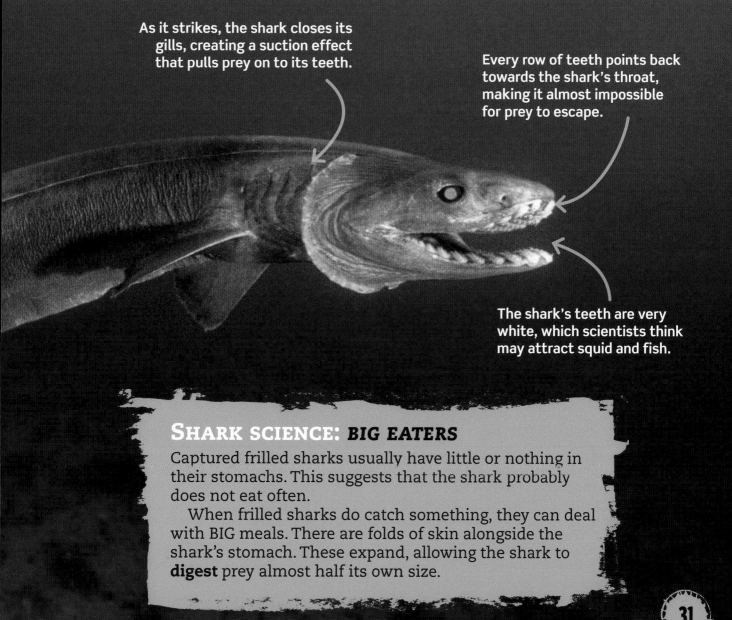

The shark's teeth are very white, which scientists think may attract squid and fish.

SHARK SCIENCE: *BIG EATERS*

Captured frilled sharks usually have little or nothing in their stomachs. This suggests that the shark probably does not eat often.

When frilled sharks do catch something, they can deal with BIG meals. There are folds of skin alongside the shark's stomach. These expand, allowing the shark to **digest** prey almost half its own size.

THRESHER SHARK

If you see a thresher shark coming towards you, you will probably think it is just an ordinary shark. If it turns sideways, though... wow!
What a tail!

There are three different types of thresher shark: common, bigeye, and **pelagic**. Common threshers are the largest, followed by bigeye and pelagic.

This thresher shark is at a "cleaning station," having tiny parasites picked off its skin by small fish.

Thresher sharks have weaker bites than most other sharks. They also have fewer teeth (usually 80, compared to a great white's 300). They do not rely on their jaws for catching prey.

Common and bigeye threshers are usually dark green or brown, so that they blend in with the bottom as they swim along hunting for prey. Pelagic threshers are usually bluish, to blend in with the open ocean.

All threshers have large eyes, and the bigeye's are among the largest of all animals. A thresher's eyes point upwards, enabling it to spot **schools** of fish swimming above.

Compared to their overall size (up to 20 ft/ 6 m), these sharks have by far the longest tail in the shark world. A thresher's tail is its biggest weapon and can be half its total length. At nearly 10 ft (3 m), it matches the world's tallest-ever man, Robert Wadlow, who was 8ft 11in (2.72 m) tall.

When the shark finds prey, it uses its tail like a whip, threshing the water to stun and even kill fish.

SHARK SCIENCE:
AN ORDER OF ODDBALLS

Scientists divide sharks into eight orders.* Threshers are from the "mackerel shark" order.

Mackerel sharks have two dorsal fins, five gill slits, and a mouth that goes back past their eyes. Apart from that, they do not always have much in common. Mackerel sharks include threshers and goblin sharks, as well as megamouth and basking sharks.

Angel sharks, bullhead sharks, carpet sharks, dogfish, ground sharks, mackerel sharks, sawsharks, and sixgill sharks

WHALE SHARK

The whale shark is the biggest shark in the ocean. In fact, it is the biggest fish of any kind. Despite its huge size, the whale shark is harmless to all but the smallest sea creatures.

The size of a double-decker bus

The biggest whale sharks are 40 ft (12 m) long—about the length of a double-decker bus. They weigh about 11 US tons (10 metric tonnes)—the same as five rhinoceroses.

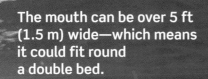

The mouth can be over 5 ft (1.5 m) wide—which means it could fit round a double bed.

PLANKTON AND KRILL

The whale shark swims along with its mouth open, scooping up plankton and krill. These tiny creatures are one of the building blocks of ocean life. They are at the bottom of the **food chain**. Without them, animals higher up the food chain cannot survive. This makes whale sharks an indicator of the health of the oceans. If there is plenty of plankton for them to eat, other creatures will have enough to eat, too..

A CRAFTY HUNTER

Whale sharks are crafty and patient. They have been seen waiting for hours until fish eggs hatch—then swooping in and gulping down the lot. Whale sharks migrate from place to place, depending on where they will find food. They have been tracked making enormous journeys of more than 7,500 miles (12,000 km).

A shark this big could be a terrifying predator. It's a good job a whale shark's main prey is plankton, krill, and small fish.

SHARK SCIENCE: WHALE-SHARK FINGERPRINTS!

Sharks do not have fingerprints, of course: they do not have fingers. But every whale shark still has its own personal ID.

Whale sharks all have a pattern of spots and stripes on their backs. No two sharks have exactly the same pattern. Scientists use the patterns to identify different sharks and track their movements.

SAWSHARK

The sawshark is a weird-looking shark indeed. Its saw is SO long that it looks as though it would get in the way of feeding, rather than helping it catch prey.

HUNTING TECHNIQUE

A sawshark's prey consists of small fish, **crustaceans,** and squid. It hunts in shallow water near the coast, in bays, and **estuaries**. The sawshark begins its hunt by searching for the tiny electrical signals of its prey's heartbeat. Once it senses them, it knows there is something buried in the sand.

This Japanese saw shark is a little over 3 ft 3 in (1 m) long. It hunts prey on the sandy seabed.

Killing prey

Once the sawshark detects prey, its saw swings into action. The shark sweeps it quickly back and forth. The prey either tries to escape and gets sliced up, or stays where it is and gets sliced up. The shark gobbles down the stunned, injured, or dead fish.

Sensors under the shark's saw detect tiny electrical charges given off by hidden fish (see page 19, Shark Science).

Some sensors detect tiny movements in the water.

Long, whiskery barbels contain lots of touch- and smell-sensitive cells, allowing the shark to feel and sniff out prey.

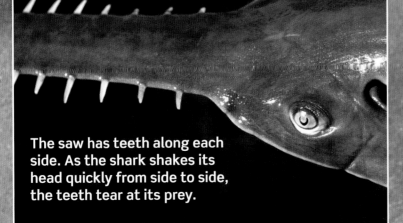

The saw has teeth along each side. As the shark shakes its head quickly from side to side, the teeth tear at its prey.

SHARK SCIENCE:
BABY SAWSHARKS

When baby longnose sawsharks are born, their teeth are folded back into their snouts.

This prevents the baby sharks' mother being cut to pieces while she is giving birth. Within hours, the babies' longest teeth have sprung forward, ready for action. Smaller teeth then begin to grow between the longer ones.

HORN SHARK

The horn shark belongs to a group called bullhead sharks. These get their name from their large, squarish heads—which look like they could give you a nasty bash!

The horn shark is named after the horn-like ridges above its eyes.

Some horn sharks eat so many purple sea urchins that their teeth are dyed purple.

For its size, about 3 ft 3in (1 m), this shark has one of the most powerful bites in the animal world. This is very useful for crushing hard-shelled prey.

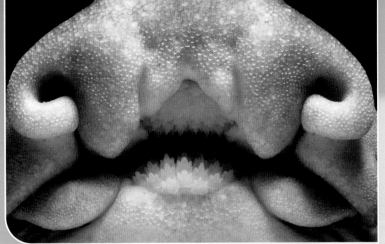

Small, hooked front teeth are for grabbing prey. Larger, flat side teeth are for grinding up food.

HUNTING AND HIDING

Despite appearances, the horn shark is not likely to be aggressive in any way. In fact it is very shy, and mostly stays within a small home territory.

The horn shark hunts at night. During the day, it hides in a cave or crevice, and usually has a preferred hiding place. After a night's hunting, it returns to the same spot, day after day, for years.

This shark does not like light at all. If you shine a bright light on one at night, it usually sinks to the bottom and lies there motionless, pretending not to exist.

BOTTOM WALKER

Molluscs, crustaceans, starfish, and sea urchins make up the horn shark's diet. It is a fairly poor swimmer, and instead of swimming, it uses its **pectoral fins** to "walk" along the bottom looking for food.

SHARK SCIENCE:
HORN SHARK BREEDING

Horn sharks do not give birth to live young. They lay eggs, shaped like a cone.

The female wedges her egg cones into tight places in the rocky sea bottom. This makes it difficult for predators to find and eat the eggs before the baby horn sharks have hatched.

EPAULETTE SHARK

If there's one thing most people really do NOT want to hear, it's that some sharks can walk on land. At least one shark can do just that, though.

ROCK-POOL HUNTING

The epaulette shark lives in shallow water near coral reefs. As the **tide** drops, parts of the reef are left exposed to the air. Rock pools are formed, and these are where the epaulette shark hunts. The fish trapped in the pools are unable to escape to sea until the tide rises again. They are easy pickings for the shark.

REEF-CRAWLER

The epaulette's plan is to be left in a rock pool with a lot of tasty fish. Sometimes, though, the plan goes wrong. The shark miscalculates, and finds itself stranded on dry reef. When this happens, the epaulette can use its strong pectoral fins to crawl across the reef to water. If the distance is too far, the shark lies still and waits for the tide to rise again.

Like the horn shark (see page 38), the epaulette moves about partly by crawling along the sea floor using its pectoral fins.

Epaulettes sometimes eat crustaceans. When they do, their sharp teeth flatten and become shell-crushing plates.

The shark's epaulettes are just about where its shoulders would be—if sharks had shoulders.

An epaulette is a decoration on the shoulder of a jacket. The epaulette shark gets its name from the spot of black on its side.

Epaulette sharks are common in the seas around Australia's Great Barrier Reef.

SHARK SCIENCE:
A FISH OUT OF WATER

Sharks are a kind of fish, and fish need to be in water to breathe. So how does the epaulette shark survive when it is stranded on a dry reef?

The answer is that the shark powers down its brain, and slows its heart rate and breathing. This means it uses far less oxygen. As a result, epaulettes can survive 60 times longer without oxygen than a human.

GHOST SHARK

When is a shark not a shark? When it's a ghost shark! Technically, a ghost shark is not a shark at all. It's a chimera.

The ghost shark hunts in the deep ocean, haunting the depths where light never reaches.

Long tail that gave ghost sharks one of their other names: ratfish

CHIMERAS AND SHARKS

Chimeras and sharks are close relatives. Both have a skeleton made of tough cartilage, instead of bone. They even look alike: ghost sharks look similar to sharks from the bullhead order, such as the horn shark (page 38).

Flat plates in mouth for grinding up molluscs found on the seabed

Large pectoral fins used for swimming

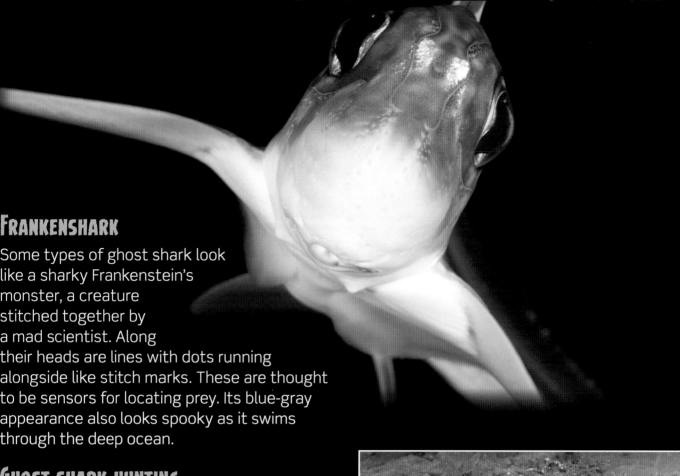

FRANKENSHARK

Some types of ghost shark look like a sharky Frankenstein's monster, a creature stitched together by a mad scientist. Along their heads are lines with dots running alongside like stitch marks. These are thought to be sensors for locating prey. Its blue-gray appearance also looks spooky as it swims through the deep ocean.

GHOST-SHARK HUNTING

Ghost sharks are too rare to eat—but even taking photos of them is a tricky job. They live in the deepest ocean, and there are hardly any around. You could wait underwater for weeks before one swam by. In 2009, for example, a crew filming life on the sea bottom caught a ghost shark on camera—but only by accident!

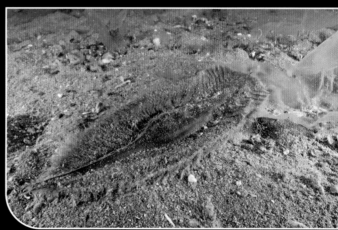

Ghost shark egg

SHARK SCIENCE: CHIMERAS

How do sharks differ from chimeras?

One obvious difference is that instead of having teeth like a true shark, chimeras have toothy plates in their mouths. Unlike a shark's teeth, these plates are not replaced again and again throughout the ghost shark's life.

Also, chimeras swim mainly using their pectoral fins like wings, while a shark swishes its tail from side to side.

WOBBEGONG

This shark's extraordinary appearance makes it an effective hunter. It waits patiently in ambush on the seabed—and when unwary food swims by, it strikes like lightning!

No one in this school of little fish has spotted the wobbegong they are swimming past!

The wobbegong's sharp teeth are shaped so that anything it bites cannot wriggle off. Once a wobbegong grabs hold, it does not like to let go.

A wide, flat body is perfect for hiding on the sea floor, pretending to be a rock. The shark's dorsal fins are set far back from its mouth

MASTERS OF DISGUISE

In the shark world, the master of disguise is the wobbegong. There are 12 different kinds of wobbegong. All are camouflaged brown, gray, and yellow, making them almost impossible to spot on the sea bottom. Some have frills around their jaws that look just like seaweed. To a fish looking for shelter, or perhaps some food to nibble, these frills look welcome—right up until the wobbegong pounces!

ACCIDENTAL ATTACKER

Unfortunately, it's not only fish that find wobbegongs hard to spot. Around Australia's busy coastline, people sometimes accidentally tread on a wobbegong that's lying disguised on the bottom. Sometimes the shark just swims off, but once in a while it bites back.

SHARK SCIENCE:
SMALL EATERS

Wobbegongs only need to eat every three or four days. Since they do not swim much, their bodies do not need a lot of energy from food. So wobbegongs have developed with a slow **metabolism**.

The dangling frills are called "dermal lobes." They are part of the wobbegong's disguise, and they also attract prey.

GREENLAND SHARK

The Greenland shark is one of the longest-lived creatures on Earth. It can easily survive up to 200 years. Some are thought to have reached double that age!

ARCTIC HUNTER

This shark lives in the cold seas of the subarctic. It swims to depths where sunlight never reaches. It grows as large as a pickup truck, and is a fearsome hunter. Though the shark mostly eats fish, it is also thought to attack seals and small whales. Greenland sharks have even been seen grabbing reindeer and other animals that come too close to the edge of the ice.

The Greenland shark is one of the largest sharks. At over 20 ft (6 m) long, it is a similar size to the great white.

ADAPTED FOR THE COLD

The Greenland shark is specially adapted to life in the coldest seas. As the temperature drops, it moves more and more slowly. The shark is not quite hibernating, because it never stops swimming. It is shutting down its body as much as possible, to save energy in the cold. Though able to make short bursts of speed, it is usually slow-moving.

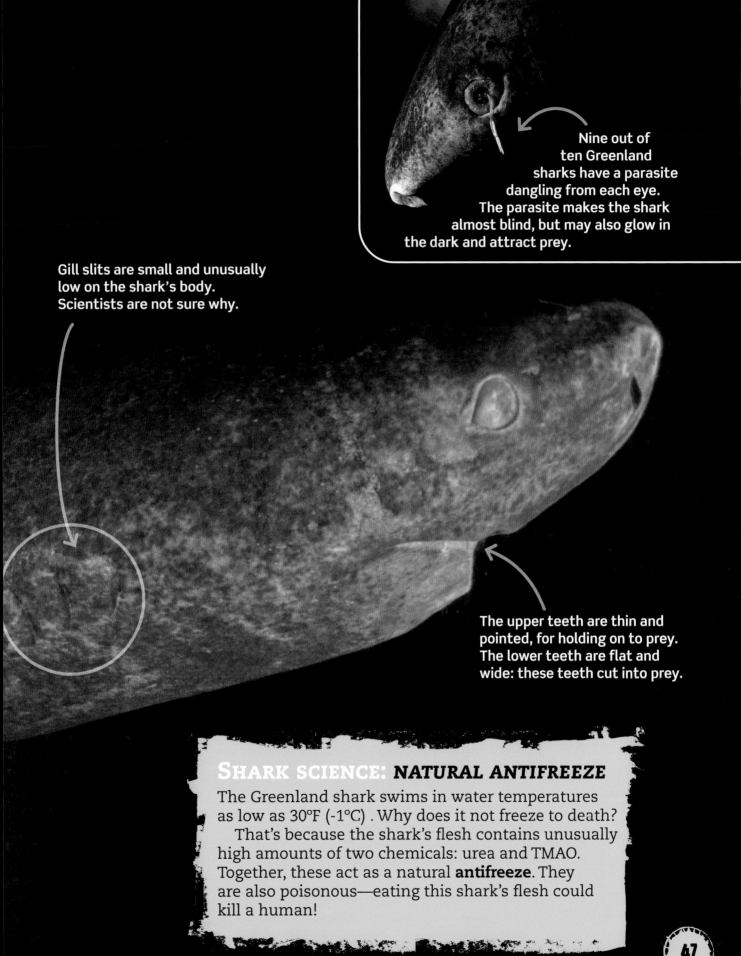

Nine out of ten Greenland sharks have a parasite dangling from each eye. The parasite makes the shark almost blind, but may also glow in the dark and attract prey.

Gill slits are small and unusually low on the shark's body. Scientists are not sure why.

The upper teeth are thin and pointed, for holding on to prey. The lower teeth are flat and wide: these teeth cut into prey.

SHARK SCIENCE: NATURAL ANTIFREEZE

The Greenland shark swims in water temperatures as low as 30°F (-1°C) . Why does it not freeze to death?

That's because the shark's flesh contains unusually high amounts of two chemicals: urea and TMAO. Together, these act as a natural **antifreeze**. They are also poisonous—eating this shark's flesh could kill a human!

SHARK EXTREMES

Sharks come in many different shapes and sizes. They range in size from enormous to tiny. They live in deep oceans and shallow waters, far out to sea and in rivers. Here are just a few extremes of the shark world.

BIGGEST

The biggest shark, and world's biggest fish, is the whale shark, and the largest recorded specimen was 43 ft (13.2 m) long. The second biggest is the basking shark, which can reach more than 30 ft (9.1 m) long.

DEEPEST

The cow shark (also called the bluntnose sixgill shark) is an amazingly adaptable hunter. Young cow sharks sometimes hunt in very shallow water, but adults have been found as far down as 8,200 ft (2,500 m). Other deep-sea sharks include goblin, ghost, and frilled sharks.

SMALLEST

The dwarf lanternshark grows to no more than 8.3 in (21 cm)—about as long as an adult's hand. It lives in deep, dark waters off the coast of South America. The shark gets its name from being bioluminescent: it glows in the dark as a way of attracting food.

FASTEST

The fastest shark is the shortfin mako. Measuring how fast a shark swims in the open ocean is difficult, but it has been claimed that makos can swim at over 43 mph (70 km/h)—plenty fast enough to break the speed limit in most cities.

MOST DANGEROUS

The most dangerous shark, based on statistics from the Florida Museum of Natural History in the USA, is the great white. By 2017, great whites were thought to have killed at least 80 people since records began in 1580. Next came tiger sharks (31 people) and bull sharks (27 people).

HOTTEST

Scientists got a shock when they sent an underwater camera down off the coast of Fiji to view an active undersea volcano. Among the creatures swimming around inside the volcano's crater were two kinds of shark: scalloped hammerheads and silky sharks. They would not survive an actual eruption, but were able to swim in the ash-clouded, acidic water.

3. SHARK ATTACKS

SHARK ATTACKS: THE REALITY

For most people, the thought of being attacked by a shark is terrifying. Fortunately, though, shark attacks are extremely rare.

THE CHANCES OF BEING BITTEN

Most sharks are harmless. You are far more likely to have a car crash on your way to the beach than be bitten by a shark when you get there. Even being struck by lightning is more likely.

There are about 450 different shark species. Of these...

Only **13 species** (2.9 per cent) are suspected of having killed humans.

Most sharks are harmless, but in some places there is a risk of meeting dangerous ones. This sign on a California beach warns people of fatal shark attacks here in the past.

WARNING
(¡Precaución!)
FATAL SHARK ATTACKS
(Ataque de Tiburon Fatal)
SWIM/SURF AT YOUR OWN RISK
(Nade bajo su propio riesgo)

KEEP AWAY FROM MARINE WILDLIFE
(No se acerque a los animales marinos)

IDENTIFYING THE ATTACKER

Only great white, bull, and tiger sharks are known ever to have killed more than 10 people. But it is not always certain what kind of shark is the **perpetrator** of an attack. Oceanic whitetip sharks are thought to have killed many shipwrecked sailors (see pages 54–55). But without surviving witnesses, oceanic whitetips cannot be included in shark attack statistics.

Only **seven species** (1.6 per cent) are thought to have killed more than one person.

Only **three species** (0.67 per cent) are known to have killed more than 10 people.

A great white shark attacks a young seal. This is the world's most dangerous species. Even so, great whites are thought to have killed fewer than one person per year over the last 100 years.

SHARK SCIENCE: SPECIALIST TEETH

Each shark species has teeth that are adapted to the kind of prey it hunts. As sharks hunt almost anything that can be eaten, there are lots of different kinds of shark teeth.

Sharks' teeth also frequently fall out and are replaced with new ones from behind. Some sharks are thought to grow tens of thousands of teeth in a lifetime

THE JERSEY SHORE MAN-EATER

New York

Date: July 1-12, 1916
Location: off New Jersey, USA

Matawan
July 12

In 1916, shark attacks off the East Coast of the USA left four people dead. The attacks marked the beginning of our modern terror of sharks.

Spring Lake
July 6

ATTACK 1: BEACH HAVEN

On Saturday July 1, vacationer Charles Vansant decided to go for a swim before dinner. Soon after entering the water, Vansant began shouting for help. A large shark had attacked his legs. A lifeguard and another man pulled him to shore, followed by the shark—but within minutes Vansant had died.

Philadelphia

Beach Haven
July 1

ATTACK 2: SPRING LAKE

Five days after Vansant's death, Charles Bruder was swimming 320 ft (100 m) offshore when he too was attacked. There was so much blood in the water that a woman told lifeguards she thought a red canoe had capsized. The lifeguards rowed out to help, but Bruder died on the way back to land.

Attacks 3, 4 and 5: Matawan

Six days later, sea captain Thomas Cottrell spotted a shark in Matawan Creek. He tried to warn people, but they did not believe sharks swam in rivers. Minutes later, 11-year-old Lester Stilwell was attacked and killed by the shark. When townspeople went to find Lester's body, Watson Fisher was also attacked and later died.

Minutes later, Joseph Dunn was swimming off a dock with friends when word of the attacks reached them. As he climbed out of the water, the shark bit his leg. After a tug of war between his friends and the shark, Joseph was pulled from the water and survived.

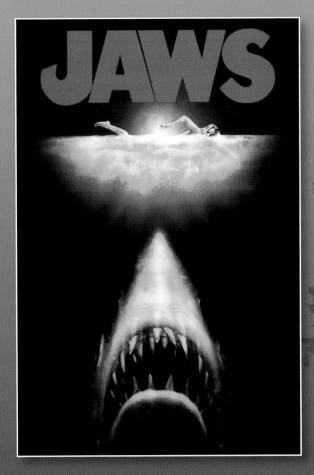

Shark science: WHICH SHARK LAUNCHED THE ATTACKS?

It is not certain what species carried out the Jersey Shore attacks. There are two main suspects:

- A bull shark (bull sharks regularly swim in fresh water)
- A young great white

On July 14, two days after the last attacks, an 8-ft 10-in (2.7-m) great white was caught and killed close to Matawan Creek. The attacks stopped, making it likely that this was the shark responsible.

The hit 1975 movie *Jaws*, about a killer shark off the coast of Long Island, was inspired by the Jersey Shore man-eater.

THE INDIANAPOLIS SHIPWRECK

Date: July 30, 1945
Location: Philippine Sea

Just after midnight, the US Navy ship *Indianapolis* was sunk by torpedoes from a Japanese submarine. About 900 of the crew ended up in the water, drifting in groups in their life jackets.

SECRET MISSION

The *Indianapolis* had been on a secret mission. It had delivered an atomic bomb, which in a few days would be used to attack the Japanese city of Hiroshima. The mission was so secret that it was days before rescue arrived. As the shipwrecked sailors waited, sharks began to gather and attack them.

The oceanic whitetip grows to 13 ft (4 m) and weighs up to 370 lb (170 kg).

Long pectoral fins give the whitetip part of its Latin name: longimanus or "long hands." The shark's English name comes from the white tips on its fins.

The oceanic whitetip, a strong, thick-bodied shark, is thought to have attacked the crew of the Indianapolis.

Rescued survivors from the USS Indianapolis receive medical help on the island of Guam.

CAUTIOUS BUT DETERMINED

Oceanic whitetips are cautious hunters, especially when attacking large prey. If they come close to investigate, it may be possible to beat them away. The danger has not gone away, though. Whitetips continue to shadow or circle their prey until another opportunity to attack occurs.

About 900 crew members survived the sinking of the *Indianapolis*. Many then died from exposure and dehydration, as well as from shark attacks. Only 321 were rescued alive, and only 317 of them survived. No one is certain how many of the dead were eaten by sharks, but it is thought to have been at least 150 people.

The powerful jaw has wide triangular teeth above for slicing into prey, and smaller pointed teeth below for a good grip.

SHARK SCIENCE:
WHAT CAUSED THE ATTACK

Oceanic whitetip sharks usually hunt alone, but they are known to gather quickly at possible food sources—including shipwrecks.

Any oceanic whitetips within a couple of miles are attracted by the noise of a ship going down. As they swim nearer, the sharks begin to smell the sailors in the water. Once they are really close, the sharks can see their victims.

Shark Expert Erich Ritter

Date: April 11, 2002
Location: Bahamas, Caribbean Sea

Shark expert Dr Erich Ritter had a theory about shark attacks. He thought that sharks were attracted by fast human heartbeats. Therefore, lowering your heartbeat would keep you safe.

THEORY IN ACTION

Ritter regularly swam with bull sharks, or stood chest-deep in water where they were feeding. He used special exercises to slow down his breathing and heartbeat. Bull sharks are among the most dangerous sharks. Ritter was sometimes **bumped** by the sharks and had to leave the water, but until 2002 he had never been bitten.

Bull sharks have attacked humans at least 100 times. They get their name from their short snouts, fierce nature, and habit of butting victims before biting.

At Carbrook golf course in Australia, balls lost in the water stay lost! Bull sharks patrol the lake, having first swum there during a flood and become trapped.

BULL SHARK

RITTER BITTEN

In 2002, Dr Ritter was explaining his theory to a TV presenter. The two men were standing waist-deep in water, surrounded by bull sharks. To show how well the theory worked, raw fish had been put in the water for the sharks to feed on. Unfortunately, a short time into the interview one of the sharks bit Dr Ritter on the lower leg.

Ritter and the interviewer quickly got out of the water, and Ritter was rushed to hospital. He survived, but spent weeks in hospital and lost a large piece of his calf. He is unlikely ever to be able to use his foot properly again, because the shark bit off so much muscle.

SHARK SCIENCE: WHAT CAUSED THE ATTACK

Some shark experts had feared Dr Ritter would eventually be bitten. They thought this for two main reasons:

1) Deliberately spending a lot of time in the water with dangerous sharks makes an attack more likely.

2) Dr Ritter went into the water with bare legs. Underwater, skin can look similar to some kinds of fish. Hungry, curious sharks are attracted to them, and they may take a bite to see if it's food.

SURFER BETHANY HAMILTON

Date: October 31, 2003
Location: Hawaii, Pacific Ocean

One October morning in 2003, 13-year-old Bethany Hamilton went surfing off Tunnels Beach in Hawaii. With her were her friend Alana Blanchard, Alana's brother, and their father Holt.

THE ATTACK

The surfers paddled out into the warm Hawaiian waters to catch some fun waves. At around 7.30 a.m., Bethany was lying on her surfboard with her left arm dangling in the water. Seconds later, a shark had bitten her arm off. It happened so fast that none of the other surfers in the water even noticed.

THE RESCUE

Holt Blanchard knew that many shark-attack victims bleed to death. He used his surfboard **leash** as a **tourniquet** to slow Bethany's bleeding. The surfers then began the long 650-ft (200-m) paddle back to shore, which they managed in safety.

Bethany was rushed to hospital. There, in a strange coincidence, her father was waiting for an operation. Bethany took her Dad's place on the operating table. The wound was closed up and, despite losing 60 per cent of her blood, Bethany survived.

Bethany Hamilton was attacked by a tiger shark like this one. Tiger sharks haunt warm, tropical waters.

In 2011, a film called *Soul Surfer* was released. It tells the story of the attack on Bethany and her return to surfing. The film is based on Bethany's book of the same name, which came out in 2004.

AFTER THE ATTACK

Soon after the attack, a group of fishermen caught a 24-ft (4.3-m) tiger shark close by. Experts compared the shark's mouth with the bite marks on Bethany's surfboard. It was the shark that had attacked her.

Once she had recovered, Bethany got back on her surfboard. Since then she has won the national surfing championship, as well as contests at Pipeline, Hawaii— one of the world's toughest waves.

She may have lost her arm to a shark in 2003, but Bethany Hamilton still rips! Here she is competing in a surfing contest in Hawaii in 2008.

SHARK SCIENCE:
WHAT CAUSED THE ATTACK

Reports said that when Bethany was attacked, there were sea turtles in the water. Tiger sharks hunt turtles, so they may have attracted this particular shark.

Once there, the shark saw the surfer's pale arm in the water. It probably bit her thinking her arm was a fish.

Surfer Elio Canestri

Date: April 12, 2015
Location: off Réunion, Indian Ocean

BULL SHARK

Taking to the water around the island of Réunion poses a huge risk. Between 1996 and 2015, there were 28 shark attacks there. In 14 of the attacks, the victim died.

Attacks on Réunion

After five people had died in just two years, in 2013 the authorities decided they had to do something. Swimming and surfing were banned on many of the island's beaches. In 2014, there was only one attack, and the surfer escaped with minor injuries. But in February 2015, a swimmer was killed close to shore. All water activities were banned unless there was a shark spotter on the lookout.

The attack on Elio

On April 12, 2015, 13-year-old Elio Canestri paddled out with his friends at a surf spot called Zaigrettes. The surfers were about 160 ft (50 m) from shore when a wave came Elio's way. As he paddled to catch it, a bull shark attacked. Although a rescue boat quickly reached him, Elio did not survive. He was the seventh person to be killed by Réunion's sharks in just four years.

Bull sharks are thought to be behind almost all the attacks in the seas off Réunion.

PROTESTS IN RÉUNION

After Elio's death there were protests about people being killed in shark attacks. Two beaches were **netted** to make them safe for surfers and swimmers. Underwater lookouts armed with harpoon guns were posted. Even so, attacks have continued. By 2017, three more surfers had been attacked, but survived. Then in February 2017, yet another surfer was killed by a shark.

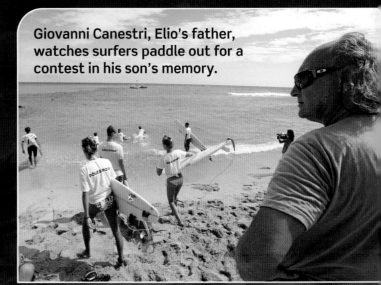

Giovanni Canestri, Elio's father, watches surfers paddle out for a contest in his son's memory.

SHARK SCIENCE: WHAT CAUSED THE ATTACKS

No one is sure why Réunion has seen so many shark attacks. There are several possible explanations:

- A new marine park created in 2007 has boosted fish numbers, so there is more for sharks to eat.
- The sale of shark meat has been banned, which means sharks are no longer caught.
- The number of reef sharks, which used to eat many of the young bull sharks, has fallen.

THE SHARK ATTACK THAT WASN'T

Date: October 30, 2004
Location: Ocean Beach, Whangarei, New Zealand

When four swimmers headed into the sea off Ocean Beach, New Zealand, it was the start of an amazing encounter with local sea life.

SWIMMING WITH DOLPHINS

In the water were Karina Cooper, Helen Slade, lifeguard Rob Howes, and his teenage daughter, Niccy. They were all members of the Whangarei Surf Lifesaving Club, out for a training swim. Suddenly, a **pod** of dolphins raced towards them. As Rob said:

"They were... turning tight circles around us, slapping the water with their tails."

One of the dolphins swam straight at Rob and Helen, before zooming underneath them. As Rob watched what the dolphin was doing, he was horrified to see a 10-ft (3-m) great white swim past. The shark headed for the other two swimmers.

If a dolphin calf is attacked by a shark, the whole pod tries to protect it.

BOTTLENOSE DOLPHIN AND CALF

Lifeguard Rob Howes safely on dry land at Ocean Beach, Whangarei

FENDING OFF THE SHARK

The dolphins diverted the shark before it could reach the two girls. Then the dolphins swam back and forward around all four humans, forming a protective barrier while the shark kept circling. The humans trod water and the dolphins stayed with them the whole time. Another lifeguard, Matt Fleet, came over in a boat to see what was going on. He dived in to join the swimmers before seeing the shark. Finally, after 40 minutes, the shark gave up and swam away.

SHARK SCIENCE:
WHAT STOPPED THE ATTACK

Bottlenose dolphins are not usually hunted by sharks, but baby dolphins are sometimes attacked. This may be why dolphins are known to gang up on sharks and fight them off.

Dolphins have been recorded protecting humans more than once. As well as the Ocean Beach lifeguards, long-distance swimmers and divers have been saved by them. Why they do this is not known.

ATTACKS IN NORTHERN CALIFORNIA

Date: 15–30 September 1984
Location: off northern California, Pacific Ocean

The coast of northern California is home to thousands of elephant seals. Great white sharks hunt elephant seals. With plenty of food around, this area is famous for its great whites.

SURFERS AND DIVERS

The seals and sharks are not alone in California's seas. The state has great surfing waves and rich ocean life. It is popular with surfers and divers, especially spearfishers. Over the years there have been many shark attacks in northern California.

During the breeding season, from January to March, there are thousands of elephant seals for sharks to hunt.

Omar Conger

On 15 September 1984, Omar Conger was out diving for **abalone** with his friend Chris Rehm. They were on the surface when, as Chris later said:

'[A] huge white shark came up, grabbed [Omar] from behind, and while shaking him violently, pulled him under the water. I never saw the shark before the attack.'

Chris pulled his friend on to a **surf mat** they had been using and swam to shore, all the time expecting the shark to reappear. They reached shore without seeing it again, but Omar had died.

Paul Parsons

Two weeks after Omar Conger died, Paul Parsons was diving for abalone. When he was underwater, he felt scared without knowing why, so he came back to the surface. His boat was 320 ft (100 m) away, so Paul decided it would be safer on the bottom and dived back down. When he surfaced a second time to get into the boat, a shark attacked. Paul fought until it released him, and was hauled into the boat. He was badly bitten but made a full recovery.

SHARK SCIENCE:
WHAT CAUSED THE ATTACKS

Both attacks happened in dangerous areas where great white sharks hunt. Several divers and kayakers have been attacked by great whites off Pigeon Point, where Omar Conger died. And Paul Parsons was the seventh person to be attacked near Tomales Point in Marin County.

How to avoid a shark attack

If you do not have a dolphin bodyguard (see pages 62—63),
what can you do to avoid being attacked by a shark?
Here are 10 tips.

 ## SWIM WITH FRIENDS...
BUT NOT A DOGGY FRIEND!

Sharks are thought to be less likely to attack
large groups of people. However, to a shark the
noise of a swimming dog is like a dinner bell,
because it sounds like an injured fish.

 ## NEVER PEE OR BLEED
IN THE WATER

Most shark experts think that pee or
blood in the water attracts sharks.
They may be able to tell that it is
not fish blood, but
hunting sharks
will still come to
investigate.

 ## CHECK OUT THE
LOCAL HISTORY

If you're in a place where sharks have
attacked before, they are probably
still out there. Stay out of the water!

 ## AVOID SUDDEN DROP-OFFS,
RIVER MOUTHS, AND CHANNELS

Great whites like to hunt in places where
shallow water suddenly gets deep. Bull
sharks haunt river mouths and deeper
channels where the water flow may bring
them fish and other food.

 AVOID NIGHTTIME... AND DAWN... AND DUSK!

Sharks hunt mostly at night, but are also active at dawn and dusk. That makes these really bad times to surf/swim/dive.

 BUY A SHARK SCARER, POSSIBLY...

Shark scarers use an electric pulse to ward off an attacking shark. (At least one person has been bitten while wearing one, though...)

DON'T SWIM IN MURKY WATER

There is less chance of you spotting a shark in murky water, and more chance of a small shark bumping into you and biting to see what you are.

BE VERY CAREFUL ABOUT SPEARFISHING

Many shark attacks have been triggered by fish wriggling on the end of a diver's spear.

WATCH THE SHARK

If a shark does appear, try to keep sight of it. Most sharks prefer to make a surprise attack on their victims.

FIGHT BACK

Many survivors report that they fought back. Shark noses, gills, and eyes are especially sensitive—though they have the disadvantage of being very close to the shark's mouth.

Shark Attacks: the chances

By now, you might have decided only to swim at the swimming pool, because it sounds as though there are sharks on the prowl looking for human victims at every beach! In reality, the chance of even seeing a shark, let alone being attacked by one, is tiny.

Sharks v. bears

In the USA, researchers have found that you are twice as likely to be killed by a bear as by a shark.

Surfers v. non-surfers

Most people (in 2016, 58 per cent) who are attacked by sharks are surfers of some kind. So, not being a surfer makes it a lot less likely you will be bitten by a shark.

Sharks v. dogs

One survey found that between 2001 and 2010, you were 33 times as likely to be killed by a dog as by a shark. The chances of being bitten, rather than killed, by a dog were even higher.

Being bitten by a shark v. drowning

Based on statistics from the year 2000, the chances of being bitten by a shark that year were 1 in 11.5 million. You would be really unlucky to be that one person out of 11.5 million. Meanwhile, the chances of drowning were 1 in 3.5 million.

Sharks v. sand

Between 1990 and 2006, one-and-a-half times as many Americans were killed by sand holes they had dug collapsing on top of them as by sharks.

In fact, there are a lot of VERY unlikely things that are still more likely to kill you than a shark: a plane crash, a train crash, a cycling accident, fireworks, heat exposure, falling over... even death by accidental poisoning is more likely.

4. SHARKS IN DANGER

HUMANS V. SHARKS

Most of us are scared of sharks, but, as you learned in the previous chapter, there is no real reason why we should be.

WHALE SHARK

For the sharks, it is a different story. Sharks have very good reason to be scared of humans. We kill millions of sharks a year. Almost all are from species that are no danger to humans.

The exact numbers are changing all the time, but the International Union for Conservation of Nature (IUCN) says that, as of 2021, 37 percent of the world's sharks and rays are now **endangered**, and their numbers have dropped by a shocking 71 percent in the last 50 years.

More than 20 types of shark are now **critically endangered**. They are soon likely to become **extinct** in the wild.

Many more are considered endangered or **vulnerable**. This means that they will become critically endangered, or even extinct, if no action is taken.

We shouldn't be scared OF sharks. We should be scared FOR them.

Critically endangered sharks in 2021 included the:

ANGEL SHARK
Mediterranean, north-eastern Atlantic
The angel shark, smoothback angel shark, and sawback angel shark are all threatened by **overfishing**.

DAGGERNOSE SHARK
Northern South America
Fishing is thought to reduce the number of daggernose sharks by 18 per cent each year. It took just 10 years for over 90% of the population to be wiped out.

GANGES SHARK
India
This river shark is threatened by overfishing and pollution. It is also losing **habitat** as dams are built on the rivers where it lives.

SCALLOPED HAMMERHEAD SHARK
Worldwide in warm waters
Overfishing is the main reason for this shark joining the critically endangered list in 2021. In some areas of the Atlantic Ocean, their populations have dropped over 95% in the last 30 years.

PONDICHERRY SHARK
China, India, Indonesia, Malaysia, Oman, Pakistan
Last offically caught and identified by experts in 1979, this species may now actually be extinct.

OCEANTIC WHITETIP SHARK
Worldwide in deep warm waters
This type of shark used to be very common, but its numbers have dropped over 70% in the last 50 years.

A whale shark swims along, gathering small sea creatures into its giant mouth as it goes.

WHO NEEDS SHARKS ANYWAY?

We ALL need sharks. They are a crucial part of life in our oceans. If sharks disappear, the balance of the ocean world is upset.

APEX PREDATORS

Many sharks are apex predators. This means that they are not usually hunted by any other animal. If the number of apex predators declines, it harms the natural environment. The examples on this page and opposite show how this can happen.

Tiger sharks are apex predators. Seabirds are part of their diet.

If the tiger shark population falls, the number of seabirds goes up.

Tuna numbers fall, affecting fish such as marlin that feed on tuna.

Fewer young tuna then grow up to replace older fish as they die.

Seabirds eat young tuna. If there are more seabirds, more young tuna get eaten.

SHARKS AND SCALLOPS

On the Atlantic coast of the USA, shark numbers have recently fallen because of overfishing. This has led to an increase in cow-nose rays, which the sharks would normally eat. Cow-nose rays love scallops, a tasty shellfish, so with more cow-nose rays there are fewer scallops.

SHARKS AND REEFS

Experts have discovered that having sharks around helps keep coral reefs healthy. When shark numbers fall, fewer large fish, such as grouper, are eaten. More grouper eat smaller fish such as parrot fish. Parrot fish are important for keeping the reef healthy, because they eat algae. Without enough parrot fish to eat algae, the reef becomes choked with algae and unhealthy.

SHARK SCIENCE: FOOD CHAIN

A food chain is a group of living things that depend on each other for food. At the bottom are small plants and animals. These are eaten by other animals. They in turn are eaten by larger, fiercer predators. At the top of the food chain are the apex predators.

SHARK FINNING

The practice of catching a shark and cutting off its fins is called shark finning. The fins are used in shark fin soup. The soup is a popular dish in Asia, especially China.

WIPING OUT THE WORLD'S SHARKS

Shark finning is wiping out the world's sharks. In some seas, so many have been killed that only 1 per cent of the population is left.

Experts worked out that, in 2006, about 38 million sharks were killed by the shark fin industry. For the same number of people to die, you would have to kill the entire populations of Switzerland, London, Rio de Janeiro, Sydney, New York City, and Los Angeles—every year.

Experts believe that shark numbers have fallen by more than half since the 1980s as a result of demand for shark fin soup.

First the shark is caught, either on a hook or in a net.

Then the shark's tail, dorsal, and pectoral fins are cut off. It is almost always still alive when this happens.

The shark is tipped back into the sea, usually still alive. Without fins it cannot swim.

The shark sinks to the sea bottom and either bleeds to death, is eaten by other sea creatures, or suffocates.

AGAINST SHARK FINNING

The trade in fins has been banned in many places. Some hotels and restaurants will not serve shark fin soup, and some airlines refuse to transport the fins. It has also become clear that shark fins can contain dangerous levels of mercury, which is harmful to humans (see page 77). As a result, demand for the fins has fallen in Hong Kong—the world's main trading place for shark fins.

Shark fins are dried and bleached (right), before being sold and becoming the main ingredient of shark fin soup (above).

SHARK SCIENCE:
SHARK SUFFOCATION

Sharks whose fins have been cut off suffocate because they cannot swim. Sharks usually breathe by taking oxygen from water flowing over their **gills**. If the shark cannot swim, there is no water flow. The shark doesn't get oxygen and slowly suffocates.

BIG-GAME AND COMMERCIAL FISHING

Sharks are not only caught for their fins. Some types of shark are caught for fun by "big-game fishermen." Sharks are also caught so that their meat can be sold.

MAKO SHARK

BIG-GAME FISHING

Catching large, powerful fish using a strong rod and reel is known as big-game fishing. People enjoy the challenge of battling against a fish that is fighting for its life. Mako sharks are popular targets among big-game fishermen. Makos fight hard and make spectacular leaps into the air as they try to escape. Great whites, blue, tiger, and bull sharks are also sometimes caught.

CATCH AND RELEASE

As the phrase suggests, "catch and release" is catching a fish, then letting it go. Today it is becoming popular with big-game fishermen. Although the fish is sometimes too exhausted to live, many fish do seem to survive. Overall, fewer sharks and other fish are killed.

COMMERCIAL FISHING

When fishermen catch sharks for their meat, they usually aim to catch particular species. For example:

- Around the north-eastern Atlantic Ocean, a type of shark called spiny dogfish is caught. It is renamed "rock salmon," "flake," or "huss," and sold in seafood restaurants.
- Salmon shark hearts are a delicacy in Japan, as are gulper shark eggs in the Maldives.
- Greenland or basking sharks are caught and **putrefied** to make "*hákarl*," a national dish of Iceland.

In some parts of the world, commercial fishing is having a disastrous effect on shark numbers. All the sharks above are **under threat**, and in some places the spiny dogfish is critically endangered.

Spiny dogfish

Greenland shark

SHARK SCIENCE:
CATCH AND RELEASE SURVIVAL

Scientists can observe what happens to a shark that has been caught and released in two ways:

1) By taking a sample of its blood—chemicals in the blood show how the fish has been affected by being caught. Many are completely exhausted
2) By fitting a "pinger"—its signal shows whether the fish is still moving around and therefore alive

By-catch

Fishermen often catch sharks in their nets without intending to. This is called "by-catch." By-catch is usually put back in the sea, dead or dying.

As this shark struggled to escape, it became more and more wrapped up in the net. Eventually it suffocated.

Drift gill nets

Drift gill nets produce a lot of by-catch. They are fishing nets that hang down in the water like a curtain. When fish swim into the net they become trapped. They cannot swim forward, and cannot escape because their gills become caught up. The nets accidentally trap many sharks, as well as turtles, dolphins, and even small whales.

Longlining

Longlining is an alternative to using drift gill nets. It makes it easier to catch exactly the right kind of fish.

A long, strong fishing line is released into the water. Dangling from the line are baited hooks, which hang at the depth where the target fish usually swim. The size of hook and bait are also designed to attract the right catch. Some unwanted fish do still get hooked, but fewer than those caught in drift nets.

This Alaskan halibut was caught on a longline set up specifically to catch this kind of fish.

Quotas

In many parts of the world, fishing boats have quotas. These are the set amounts of fish that may be caught. The quota usually specifies that the boat can catch only certain types and sizes of fish. Anything else must be thrown back. This produces a lot of by-catch.

Recently, some governments have started using a different kind of quota. The boats are allowed to keep any fish they catch. The only limit is the overall weight. The aim is to stop sharks and other fish being caught, killed, and dumped in the sea.

SHARK SCIENCE:
SHARK POISON

Eating a lot of shark meat is not only bad for the ocean environment. It can also be bad for your health.

The reason is that the flesh of large sharks sometimes contains a chemical called methylmercury. This harms the human nervous system and can even cause brain damage.

PROTECTIVE NETTING

In some places, where sharks make it dangerous for swimmers and surfers, large nets are sometimes used to keep people safe.

This young tiger shark became trapped in a protective net and died.

HARMFUL NETS

The nets are deadly to sharks and other large sea creatures. They do not simply force sharks to turn away—they trap them in the same way as drift nets (see page 76). And few of those sharks caught in nets belong to species that have attacked humans. Harmless sea creatures such as turtles also get caught in the nets.

SHARK CULLS

When shark attacks happen, people sometimes demand a **cull** of dangerous sharks. After a series of attacks in Western Australia in 2014, a cull of large predatory sharks was announced. But many people felt that the sharks would be killed without cause. After pro-shark demonstrations, the authorities cancelled the cull.

People demonstrate against a planned shark cull in Western Australia. After the cull was cancelled, experts from South Africa came to advise on setting up a shark-spotting scheme (see page 79).

SHARK SPOTTERS

On some beaches that once had shark nets, an alternative system is now being used. In South Africa, shark spotters watch from high ground, using powerful binoculars to look for sharks. If they see one, they radio the beach. A warning siren goes off and everyone knows to leave the water.

On South Africa's Cape Peninsula, a flag system warns swimmers and surfers about the risk of shark attacks:

Green: spotting conditions are good

Black: spotting conditions are poor

Red: high shark alert

White: a shark has been spotted, leave the water (a warning siren also goes off)

In summer, Shark Beach in Sydney Harbour, Australia, is protected by a shark net.

SHARK SCIENCE: WARNING SIGNS

Sharks give warnings when they are about to attack. Watching how a shark swims is a good guide to whether they might strike. Among the clues are swimming with an arched back, lowering the pectoral fins, making sudden changes of direction, and charging towards prey before veering off.

SHARK TOURISM

Lots of people are fascinated by sharks, so trips to see them are popular. "Shark tourism" is not always good for the sharks, but it can bring big benefits.

DIVE TOURISM

Diving with sharks in their natural habitat is a great way to get really close to them. The shark-diving industry is worth hundreds of millions of dollars a year. To make sure there are plenty of sharks for tourists to see, several countries have set up areas where shark fishing is banned. As a result, few sharks are killed there.

CAGE DIVING

Cage diving uses a steel cage that floats just below the surface. Divers inside the cage are safe from attack, so this is a popular way to see dangerous sharks. Sometimes blood and bait are put in the water to attract the sharks. Some surfers and swimmers say this can lead to more attacks, and that it makes sharks connect humans with blood and food.

BOAT TOURISM

Almost all sharks are harmless—but most shark fans still prefer to see them from the safety of a boat. This is causing problems for some species, especially large sharks. Whale sharks in particular are damaged by boats, when parties of tourists are brought too close.

SHARK SCIENCE:
WHALE SHARK GATHERINGS

Whale sharks generally roam the world's oceans alone. Sometimes, though, many gather together in one place to feed.

The biggest gathering is off the coast of Yucatán, Mexico. In some years, the hatching of millions of tiny tuna attracts the whale sharks. In 2009, over 400 of the sharks were seen in a single day.

SHARK REPRODUCTION

Many sharks do not reproduce very quickly. This means not enough baby sharks are being born to replace the millions of adult sharks that are killed each year.

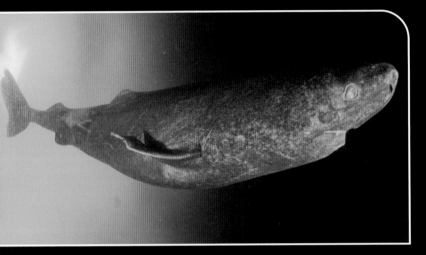

REACHING MATURITY

Most sharks take a long time to reach **maturity.** Fortunately, they do not all take as long as the Greenland shark to have young—100 years or more! Even a female great white, though, will be over 30 years old before she has pups (newborn sharks).

LONG PREGNANCIES

When sharks do start to have young, it takes a long time for the baby sharks to arrive. Female sharks are usually pregnant for 9–12 months. Many then wait two years before reproducing again.

SMALL LITTERS

A group of young sharks born together is called a litter. Sharks usually have small litters. The bigeye thresher shark, for example, has only two pups at a time. Even the blue shark, which has the biggest litters, has only about 135. This is a tiny number compared to other fish. The bluefin tuna, for example, produces up to 10 million eggs a year, although only a fraction of these survive.

A dogfish, or lesser spotted shark, hatches from an egg—often called a "mermaid's purse."

The sand tiger shark will eat young sharks if it can catch them.

A DANGEROUS WORLD

For newborn sharks, the world is a more dangerous place than ever. There are fewer safe nursery areas (see page 84), and many young sharks end up as by-catch in fishing nets. This means that fewer sharks reach an age where they can reproduce. Overall, shark numbers fall as a result.

SHARK SCIENCE: SHARK PERFUME

Many sharks are solitary and may be far away from a possible mate. When they are ready to breed, female sharks release special chemicals into the water. If a male shark from the same species gets a sniff of this perfume, it heads in the female's direction.

Shark nurseries

A nursery is a place where young sharks spend time while they are growing up. The youngsters are not very good at defending themselves, so the nursery has to be somewhere safe.

Estuaries and mangroves

Many sharks have their young in shallow-water nurseries, where there are plenty of places to hide from larger predators. The young sharks also need a supply of small fish to eat (as shown here). Estuaries—the mouths of rivers where the water is salty—make good shark nurseries. There are often weeds and other plants, rocks, and docks that provide shelter. **Mangrove** forests are also places of safety. The baby sharks can hide—and hunt—among the tangled mangrove roots.

Space is tight among the mangrove roots. When baby sharks grow larger, it is time for them to move on.

This blacktip reef shark cruising through the mangroves is a youngster. When it grows larger, it will hunt farther out to sea.

This hornshark egg case has a beautiful spiral shape.

Threats to shark nurseries

One problem for sharks is that their nurseries are slowly disappearing. Estuaries are often very beautiful, so they are popular places for people to live. Each year, more new homes and marinas are built along estuaries. Around the world, mangrove forests are also cut down to make way for shrimp farms and salt farms.

If their nurseries continue to disappear, shark numbers will fall even if humans stop killing millions of sharks each year. With fewer safe places, more young sharks will die before they reach adulthood.

SHARK SCIENCE: HATCHED OR BORN

Baby sharks arrive in the world in two different ways. Some hatch from eggs laid by the female. The eggs are often shaped to be wedged into narrow spaces, where predators cannot reach them.

Most sharks develop inside their mother and are born ready to swim off. These mini-predators are ready to start hunting right away. But because they are so small, they are also a tasty snack for other predators, so few make it to adulthood.

OCEAN POLLUTION

For many years, humans have been polluting
the sea with chemicals and waste.
This ocean pollution is making
it harder for sharks to survive.

Tags enable scientists
to monitor sharks and
their movements.

*Off the state
of New Jersey, USA,
shortfin mako sharks
have been found to
contain dangerous
levels of the chemical
methylmercury.*

CHEMICAL POLLUTION

Each year, more of our chemicals get into the sea. For example,
farm fertilizers are washed off the land by rain and flow into
rivers. The rivers carry these chemicals to the sea.

Some of the chemicals are toxic (poisonous). Sharks found
with these substances in their bodies include:

- Young great whites with high levels of DDT, a poisonous
  chemical that affects the shark's ability to breathe and the
  flow of blood around its body
- Greenland sharks with large amounts of PCBs (chemicals
  banned in the USA in 1979, and internationally in 2001);
  PCBs may affect the shark's health, including its ability to
  reproduce and the development of young sharks
- Sharks with mercury and lead contamination: their flesh
  has up to 10 times the levels considered safe to eat

Some areas of the seabed off California contain large amounts of the toxic chemical DDT. The DDT has been there since the 1970s and is still being *absorbed* by fish—including sharks.

SHORTFIN MAKO SHARK

CARBON DIOXIDE

Today, our oceans contain increasing amounts of carbon dioxide. This is affecting sharks and other sea life. Scientists are not certain what the long-term effects will be. There is some evidence that it makes it harder for sharks to smell prey. They change their hunting patterns and swim long distances looking for cleaner water.

SHARK SCIENCE: CARBON DIOXIDE IN THE OCEANS

Oceans absorb carbon dioxide from the air. The amount in the air is increasing. In 1950, it was already the highest ever: just over 300 parts per million. Since then, it has risen to over 400 parts per million.

The extra carbon dioxide came from burning fossil fuels: coal, oil, and natural gas. These fuels contain carbon dioxide. When they are burned, it is released into the air.

The catshark has been used to study how carbon dioxide affects the way sharks behave.

SAVING OUR SHARKS

Although finning and other threats are making life very difficult for sharks, things are not all bad. Recently, there have been some changes that will help protect them.

This reef shark has been tagged by a Caribbean shark research project. The simple tag will allow scientists to identify the shark if they come across it again.

UNDERSTANDING SHARKS

Publicity for sharks can play a big part in saving them. It helps people understand that sharks are crucial to the life of our oceans. For example, one of the best-known sharks is the great white. As the understanding of this shark has increased, more people have become interested in its **conservation**. Great white numbers are now rising in some areas. In 2009, just five great whites were spotted off the coast of Cape Cod, USA. By 2014 it was 80. Two years later, the number had risen to 147.

THE FIGHT AGAINST FINNING

Finning is the biggest single threat to sharks. In 2013, countries around the world agreed to restrict trade in oceanic whitetip, porbeagle, and three hammerhead species. Also in 2013, the EU banned shark finning by its boats anywhere in the world. Elsewhere in 2015, laws were confirmed to ban trade in shark fins in 10 US states. The following year, the state of Rhode Island also banned the trade in shark fins.

NET HAZARDS

Steps have been taken to stop so many sharks being accidentally caught in nets. On many beaches, shark nets are being replaced by shark spotters. Out at sea, fishermen sometimes use large floating objects to attract fish. If these are made with netting, they can entangle sharks. New net-free versions prevent this happening.

SHARK SCIENCE:
SHARKS ONLINE

You no longer have to follow a shark in real life to know what it is up to. Some sharks have their own social media!

Several great whites have been tagged with GPS devices. News of where they are goes out on their Twitter accounts.

GLOSSARY

abalone
shellfish that is prized for its taste

absorb
take in or soak up through the surface and into the inside

antifreeze
liquid that stops another liquid from freezing solid

apex predator
an animal that is not hunted by any other animal

bait ball
a ball of numerous fish all swimming around and around close together. Forming a bait ball is a stratergy used by schools of fish against predators

barb
spike with a backward-pointing hook that lodges in skin

bumped
being nudged or butted by a shark's snout

cage diving
observing sharks underwater from inside a metal cage, which protects the diver from attack

carnivorous (noun: carnivore)
an animal that only eats other animals

cartilage
strong, rubbery tissue that forms a shark's skeleton instead of bone; it makes sharks both lighter in weight and more flexible for their size than other fish

conservation
keeping the natural world safe, so that animals and environments do not disappear

critically endangered
the International Union of Conservation for Nature (IUCN) category for species facing an extremely high risk of extinction

crustacean
animal with a shell and jointed limbs, such as a crab, lobster, or shrimp

cull
deliberate killing of animals to reduce their population

delicacy
food that is particularly tasty and a special treat

digest
to break down food so that it can be used by the body

dorsal fin
fin on a fish's back

endangered
the International Union of Conservation for Nature (IUCN) category for species facing a high risk of extinction.

estuary
wide, shallow area of salty water where a river meets the sea

extinct
without a single living example

food chain
group of living things that depend on each other for food

fossil
remains of an ancient plant or animal contained in rock or resin.

fresh water
non-salty water in rivers and lakes

gill
body part that allows a fish to breathe; the gills take oxygen from water in the same way human lungs take oxygen from air

habitat
natural home of a plant or animal

immune system
body system that allows living things to fight off disease

juvenile
young and not yet fully grown

leash
strong, stretchy cord that attaches a surfer's leg to their surfboard

mangrove
a type of tree that grows along the edge of salty water in hot places

maturity
age when a living thing is physically able to produce young

metabolism
the chemical workings of the body, for example, food digestion

mollusc
animal with a soft body inside a hard shell, such as a snail, mussel, or octopus

naturalist
old name for someone interested in the world of nature. A naturalist was an early kind of scientist

netted
protected by a long net hanging down in the water, which traps dangerous sharks before they get close to shore

nutritional
providing the ingredients needed for health and growth

orca
largest member of the dolphin family, also known as a killer whale

overfishing
catching so many fish that their number drops to dangerously low levels, so they cannot be replaced

pectoral fin
fin on the sides of a fish's body

pelagic
inhabiting the deep, open ocean, a long way from land

perpetrator
someone who does something illegal or harmful to others

pod
group of dolphins or whales

pollution
harming or poisoning an environment with toxic substances and materials

pore
tiny opening in the skin

putrefied
allowed to rot

retina
layer of light-sensitive cells at the back of the eye

school
large group of the same kind of fish swimming together

shoal
large group of fish swimming together

surf mat
small inflatable mat, about 3 ft (1 m) long and 1 ft 6 in (0.5 m) wide

tag
identification label, which may give off a signal so the shark can be tracked

tide
rise and fall in the level of the sea, which happens regularly twice a day

tourniquet
cord or bandage tied tightly around an arm or leg to stop it bleeding

under threat
general term for species that face some kind of danger to their survival

vulnerable
the International Union of Conservation for Nature (IUCN) category for species that will become endangered if their situation does not improve

ABOUT THE AUTHOR

Paul Mason is a prolific author of children's books, many award-nominated, on such subjects as 101 ways to save the planet, vile things that go wrong with the human body, and the world's looniest inventors. Many take off via surprising, unbelievable or just plain revolting facts. Today, he lives at a secret location on the coast of Europe, where his writing shack usually smells of drying wetsuit (he's a former international swimmer and a keen surfer).